The Politics of Identity

Examining the Impact of Culture and Diversity on Governance

Craig Dean

The presentation of the information is without contract or any type of guarantee assurance. The trademarks that are used are without any consent, and the publication of the trademark is without permission or backing by the trademark owner. All trademarks and brands within this book are for clarifying purposes only and are the owned by the owners themselves, not affiliated with this document.

Table of Contents

Chapter 1

Introduction to Identity Politics

The Rise of Identity Politics

Identity politics has emerged as a defining force in contemporary governance, shaping the way individuals and groups engage with political systems. This rise can be traced back to a confluence of historical, social, and technological factors that have amplified the voices of marginalized communities and brought issues of identity to the forefront of political discourse. Understanding the rise of identity politics requires an exploration of its roots, its evolution, and the key theories that underpin its current manifestations.

The seeds of identity politics were sown in the civil rights movements of the mid-20th century, where marginalized groups began to organize around shared experiences of oppression and discrimination. These movements laid the groundwork for a new form of political engagement, one that prioritized the lived experiences and identities of individuals over traditional class-based politics. The feminist movement, the LGBTQ+ rights movement, and the fight for racial equality all contributed to the development of identity politics, each highlighting the unique challenges faced by different communities.

As these movements gained momentum, they began to challenge the dominant narratives that had long shaped political discourse. The notion that politics could be understood solely through the lens of economic class was increasingly called into question, as activists argued that issues of race, gender, sexuality, and other aspects of identity were equally important in shaping individuals' experiences and opportunities. This shift in focus marked a significant departure from traditional political ideologies, paving the way for a more nuanced understanding of power and privilege.

The evolution of identity politics has been influenced by several key theories and concepts. Intersectionality, a term coined by legal scholar Kimberlé Crenshaw, has become a cornerstone of identity politics, emphasizing the interconnectedness of various forms of oppression. Intersectionality posits that individuals can experience multiple, overlapping forms of discrimination, and that these experiences cannot be fully understood in isolation. This framework has been instrumental in highlighting the complexity of identity and the need for inclusive political strategies that address the diverse needs of different communities.

Another important concept in the rise of identity politics is the idea of social identity theory, which explores how individuals derive a sense of self from their membership in social groups. This theory suggests that people are motivated to maintain a positive social identity, which can lead to in-group favoritism and out-group discrimination. In the context of identity politics, social identity theory helps explain why individuals may prioritize the interests of their own identity group over broader societal concerns, and how this can lead to political polarization.

The modern era of identity politics has been shaped by the rapid advancement of media and technology, which have transformed the way individuals engage with political issues. Social media platforms, in particular, have provided new avenues for marginalized voices to be heard, allowing individuals to connect with like-minded communities and organize around shared identities. The democratization of information has empowered individuals to challenge dominant narratives and advocate for change, but it has also contributed to the fragmentation of political discourse and the rise of echo chambers.

The role of media in the rise of identity politics cannot be overstated. Traditional media outlets have often been criticized for perpetuating stereotypes and failing to adequately represent diverse perspectives. In response, alternative media platforms have emerged, offering spaces for marginalized voices to share their stories and advocate for their rights. These platforms have played a crucial role in amplifying the voices of identity-based movements, but they have also faced challenges in navigating issues of bias and misinformation.

As identity politics continues to evolve, it has sparked significant debate and controversy. Critics argue that identity politics can lead to division and fragmentation, as individuals prioritize their own identity groups over collective societal goals. They contend that this focus on identity can detract from efforts to address broader systemic issues, such as economic inequality and climate change. Proponents, on the other hand, argue that identity politics is essential for achieving true equality and justice, as it highlights the unique challenges faced by marginalized communities and advocates for policies that address their specific needs.

The rise of identity politics has also raised important questions about the role of representation and inclusion in governance. As political systems become more diverse, there is a growing recognition of the need for policies that reflect the experiences and perspectives of all individuals, regardless of their identity. This has led to increased efforts to promote diversity and inclusion in political institutions, as well as calls for more equitable representation of marginalized groups in decision-making processes.

Despite the challenges and controversies surrounding identity politics, its rise has undeniably transformed the political landscape. It has brought issues of identity and representation to the forefront of political discourse, challenging traditional power structures and advocating for a more inclusive and equitable society. As identity politics continues to shape the future of governance, it will be essential to navigate the complexities of identity with empathy and understanding, recognizing the diverse experiences and perspectives that contribute to the rich tapestry of human society.

Historical Context and Evolution

Identity politics, as a concept and practice, has deep historical roots that have evolved over time, reflecting the changing dynamics of society and governance. To understand its current significance, one must delve into the historical context that gave rise to identity-based movements and examine how these movements have transformed over the years.

The origins of identity politics can be traced back to the struggles for civil rights and social justice that emerged in the mid-20th century. During this period, marginalized groups began to organize around shared experiences of discrimination and oppression, seeking to challenge the systemic inequalities that had long been entrenched in society. The civil rights movement in the United States, for example, was a pivotal moment in the history of identity politics, as African Americans mobilized to demand equal rights and challenge the pervasive racism that permeated every aspect of their lives.

This era also saw the rise of the feminist movement, which sought to address the systemic gender inequalities that women faced in both public and private spheres. Feminists argued that traditional political frameworks, which often prioritized economic class over other forms of identity, failed to account for the unique challenges faced by women. By organizing around their shared experiences, women were able to advocate for policies that addressed issues such as reproductive rights, workplace discrimination, and domestic violence.

As these movements gained momentum, they began to influence the broader political landscape, challenging the dominant narratives that had long shaped political discourse. The notion that politics could be understood solely through the lens of economic class was increasingly called into question, as activists argued that issues of race, gender, sexuality, and other aspects of identity were equally important in shaping individuals' experiences and opportunities. This shift in focus marked a significant departure from traditional political ideologies, paving the way for a more nuanced understanding of power and privilege.

The evolution of identity politics has been shaped by several key theories and concepts that have emerged over the years. One of the most influential of these is the concept of intersectionality, which was introduced by legal scholar Kimberlé Crenshaw in the late 1980s. Intersectionality emphasizes the interconnectedness of various forms of oppression, arguing that individuals can experience multiple, overlapping forms of discrimination. This framework has been instrumental in highlighting the complexity of identity and the need for inclusive political strategies that address the diverse needs of different communities.

Another important development in the evolution of identity politics is the rise of postcolonial theory, which examines the lasting impact of colonialism on contemporary societies. Postcolonial theorists argue that the legacy of colonialism continues to shape power dynamics and social hierarchies, influencing the ways in which identity is constructed and understood. By examining the historical context of colonialism, postcolonial theory provides valuable insights into the ways in which identity politics can be used to challenge and dismantle oppressive systems.

The late 20th and early 21st centuries have seen a proliferation of identity-based movements, each advocating for the rights and recognition of specific communities. The LGBTQ+ rights movement, for example, has been instrumental in challenging societal norms and advocating for policies that promote equality and inclusion. Similarly, the disability rights movement has sought to address the systemic barriers faced by individuals with disabilities, advocating for policies that promote accessibility and inclusion.

As identity politics has evolved, it has also faced significant challenges and criticisms. Some argue that identity politics can lead to division and fragmentation, as individuals prioritize their own identity groups over collective societal goals. Critics contend that this focus on identity can detract from efforts to address broader systemic issues, such as economic inequality and climate change. However, proponents argue that identity politics is essential for achieving true equality and justice, as it highlights the unique challenges faced by marginalized communities and advocates for policies that address their specific needs.

The evolution of identity politics has also been influenced by the rapid advancement of media and technology, which have transformed the way individuals engage with political issues. Social media platforms, in particular, have provided new avenues for marginalized voices to be heard, allowing individuals to connect with like-minded communities and organize around shared identities. The democratization of information has empowered individuals to challenge dominant narratives and advocate for change, but it has also contributed to the fragmentation of political discourse and the rise of echo chambers.

As identity politics continues to evolve, it has sparked significant debate and controversy. The role of representation and inclusion in governance has become a central focus, as political systems become more diverse and there is a growing recognition of the need for policies that reflect the experiences and perspectives of all individuals, regardless of their identity. This has led to increased efforts to promote diversity and inclusion in political institutions, as well as calls for more equitable representation of marginalized groups in decision-making processes.

Despite the challenges and controversies surrounding identity politics, its evolution has undeniably transformed the political landscape. It has brought issues of identity and representation to the forefront of political discourse, challenging traditional power structures and advocating for a more inclusive and equitable society. As identity politics continues to shape the future of governance, it will be essential to navigate the complexities of identity with empathy and understanding, recognizing the diverse experiences and perspectives that contribute to the rich tapestry of human society.

Key Theories and Concepts

The landscape of identity politics is shaped by a myriad of theories and concepts that provide a framework for understanding the complexities of identity and its role in political discourse. These theories offer insights into the ways in which identity is constructed, experienced, and mobilized, shedding light on the dynamics of power, privilege, and oppression. By examining these key theories and concepts, we can gain a deeper understanding of the forces that drive identity-based movements and the challenges they face.

One of the foundational theories in the study of identity politics is intersectionality, a concept that has become central to contemporary discussions of identity and social justice. Coined by legal scholar Kimberlé Crenshaw, intersectionality emphasizes the interconnectedness of various forms of oppression, arguing that individuals can experience multiple, overlapping forms of discrimination based on their race, gender, sexuality, class, and other aspects of identity. This framework challenges the notion that identity can be understood in isolation, highlighting the need for inclusive political strategies that address the diverse needs of different communities.

Intersectionality has been instrumental in shaping the discourse around identity politics, providing a lens through which to examine the complexity of individuals' experiences. By acknowledging the ways in which different forms of oppression intersect, intersectionality encourages a more nuanced understanding of identity and the ways in which it influences individuals' opportunities and challenges. This approach has been particularly important in highlighting the experiences of marginalized groups that have historically been overlooked or excluded from mainstream political discourse.

Another key concept in the study of identity politics is the notion of social constructionism, which posits that identity is not an inherent or fixed characteristic, but rather a product of social and cultural processes. According to this perspective, identity is shaped by the norms, values, and expectations of society, and is constantly being negotiated and redefined in response to changing social dynamics. This understanding of identity as fluid and dynamic challenges traditional notions of identity as stable and unchanging, opening up new possibilities for political engagement and activism.

Social constructionism has significant implications for identity politics, as it highlights the ways in which power and privilege are embedded in social structures and institutions. By examining the social and cultural processes that shape identity, social constructionism provides a framework for understanding the ways in which identity is used to maintain and reinforce systems of oppression. This perspective encourages a critical examination of the ways in which identity is constructed and mobilized, and calls for a reevaluation of the assumptions and biases that underpin political discourse.

The concept of performativity, introduced by philosopher Judith Butler, further complicates our understanding of identity by suggesting that identity is not something that individuals possess, but rather something that they perform. According to Butler, identity is constituted through repeated acts and behaviors that conform to societal norms and expectations. This performative aspect of identity challenges the notion of identity as a fixed and stable characteristic, emphasizing the ways in which identity is constantly being enacted and re-enacted in response to social and cultural pressures.

Performativity has important implications for identity politics, as it highlights the ways in which individuals navigate and negotiate their identities in response to societal expectations. By examining the performative aspects of identity, we can gain a deeper understanding of the ways in which individuals resist and challenge dominant narratives, and the strategies they use to assert their identities in the face of oppression. This perspective encourages a more dynamic and fluid understanding of identity, recognizing the ways in which individuals actively construct and reconstruct their identities in response to changing social dynamics.

The concept of hegemony, introduced by Italian Marxist theorist Antonio Gramsci, provides another important framework for understanding the dynamics of power and identity in political discourse. Hegemony refers to the ways in which dominant groups maintain their power and control by shaping the norms, values, and beliefs of society. According to Gramsci, hegemony is achieved not through force or coercion, but through the consent and acceptance of subordinate groups, who internalize and reproduce the dominant ideology.

Hegemony has significant implications for identity politics, as it highlights the ways in which power is maintained and reinforced through cultural and ideological means. By examining the ways in which dominant groups shape and control the discourse around identity, we can gain a deeper understanding of the ways in which identity is used to maintain systems of oppression. This perspective encourages a critical examination of the ways in which identity is constructed and mobilized, and calls for a reevaluation of the assumptions and biases that underpin political discourse.

The concept of cultural capital, introduced by French sociologist Pierre Bourdieu, further complicates our understanding of identity and power by highlighting the ways in which cultural knowledge and practices are used to maintain and reinforce social hierarchies. According to Bourdieu, cultural capital refers to the knowledge, skills, and cultural competencies that individuals possess, which can be used to gain social and economic advantage. This concept challenges traditional notions of power and privilege, emphasizing the ways in which cultural capital is used to maintain and reinforce systems of oppression.

Cultural capital has important implications for identity politics, as it highlights the ways in which cultural knowledge and practices are used to maintain and reinforce social hierarchies. By examining the ways in which cultural capital is used to maintain systems of oppression, we can gain a deeper understanding of the ways in which identity is constructed and mobilized in political discourse. This perspective encourages a critical examination of the ways in which cultural capital is used to maintain and reinforce systems of oppression, and calls for a reevaluation of the assumptions and biases that underpin political discourse.

The concept of agency, which refers to the capacity of individuals to act independently and make their own choices, is another important framework for understanding identity politics. Agency challenges traditional notions of power and control, emphasizing the ways in which individuals resist and challenge dominant narratives and assert their identities in the face of oppression. This perspective encourages a more dynamic and fluid understanding of identity, recognizing the ways in which individuals actively construct and reconstruct their identities in response to changing social dynamics.

Agency has significant implications for identity politics, as it highlights the ways in which individuals navigate and negotiate their identities in response to societal expectations. By examining the ways in which individuals assert their identities and resist dominant narratives, we can gain a deeper understanding of the strategies they use to challenge systems of oppression and advocate for change. This perspective encourages a more dynamic and fluid understanding of identity, recognizing the ways in which individuals actively construct and reconstruct their identities in response to changing social dynamics.

Identity Politics in the Modern Era

Identity politics has emerged as a defining feature of the modern era, shaping the contours of political discourse and influencing the dynamics of power and representation. At its core, identity politics seeks to address the ways in which individuals' identities—such as race, gender, sexuality, and class—intersect with systems of power and privilege. This approach challenges traditional political paradigms by centering the experiences and perspectives of marginalized groups, advocating for policies and practices that promote equity and justice.

The rise of identity politics can be traced back to the social movements of the 1960s and 1970s, which sought to challenge systemic inequalities and advocate for the rights of marginalized communities. These movements laid the groundwork for contemporary identity-based activism, highlighting the ways in which identity is both a source of empowerment and a site of struggle. In the modern era, identity politics has become increasingly visible, as individuals and groups mobilize around shared experiences and common goals to advocate for change.

One of the key drivers of identity politics in the modern era is the increasing recognition of the diversity and complexity of individuals' identities. As societies become more multicultural and interconnected, there is a growing awareness of the ways in which different aspects of identity intersect and influence individuals' experiences. This recognition has led to a more nuanced understanding of identity, challenging simplistic or monolithic representations and emphasizing the importance of intersectionality in political discourse.

Intersectionality, a concept that has gained prominence in recent years, highlights the interconnectedness of various forms of oppression and the ways in which they intersect to shape individuals' experiences. This framework has been instrumental in advancing identity politics, providing a lens through which to examine the complexity of individuals' identities and the ways in which they navigate systems of power and privilege. By acknowledging the diverse and intersecting nature of identity, intersectionality encourages more inclusive and equitable political strategies that address the needs of marginalized communities.

The digital age has also played a significant role in the evolution of identity politics, providing new platforms and tools for individuals and groups to organize and advocate for change. Social media, in particular, has become a powerful tool for identity-based activism, enabling individuals to connect with like-minded individuals, share their experiences, and amplify their voices. This digital landscape has democratized access to information and resources, allowing marginalized communities to challenge dominant narratives and advocate for their rights on a global scale.

However, the rise of identity politics in the digital age has also been met with challenges and backlash. Critics argue that identity politics can be divisive, emphasizing differences rather than commonalities and leading to polarization and fragmentation. This critique is often rooted in a misunderstanding of the goals and principles of identity politics, which seeks to address systemic inequalities and promote equity and justice for all individuals. By centering the experiences and perspectives of marginalized groups, identity politics challenges the status quo and calls for a reevaluation of existing power structures and systems of oppression.

Despite these challenges, identity politics continues to be a powerful force for change in the modern era, driving social and political movements that seek to address systemic inequalities and advocate for the rights of marginalized communities. From the Black Lives Matter movement to the fight for LGBTQ+ rights, identity-based activism has played a crucial role in advancing social justice and promoting equity and inclusion.

One of the key strengths of identity politics is its ability to bring attention to the lived experiences of marginalized individuals and communities, highlighting the ways in which systemic inequalities impact their lives. By centering these experiences, identity politics challenges dominant narratives and calls for a reevaluation of existing power structures and systems of oppression. This approach encourages a more inclusive and equitable political discourse, recognizing the diverse voices and perspectives that contribute to the rich tapestry of human society.

In the modern era, identity politics has also been instrumental in advancing policy changes and reforms that promote equity and justice. From advocating for affirmative action and equal pay to challenging discriminatory practices and policies, identity-based activism has played a crucial role in shaping the political landscape and advancing the rights of marginalized communities. By centering the experiences and perspectives of marginalized groups, identity politics has driven important conversations and debates around issues of representation, inclusion, and equity.

As identity politics continues to evolve in the modern era, it will be essential to navigate these dynamics with empathy and understanding, recognizing the diverse voices and perspectives that contribute to the rich tapestry of human society. By centering the experiences and perspectives of marginalized communities, identity politics challenges the status quo and calls for a reevaluation of existing power structures and systems of oppression. This approach encourages a more inclusive and equitable political discourse, recognizing the diverse voices and perspectives that contribute to the rich tapestry of human society.

The future of identity politics will likely be shaped by ongoing debates and discussions around issues of representation, inclusion, and equity. As societies continue to grapple with the complexities of identity and the dynamics of power and privilege, it will be essential to engage in open and honest conversations that recognize the diverse experiences and perspectives of individuals and communities. By centering the voices of marginalized groups and advocating for policies and practices that promote equity and justice, identity politics has the potential to drive meaningful change and advance the rights of all individuals.

The Role of Media and Technology

Media and technology have become integral components of contemporary society, influencing how we communicate, access information, and perceive the world around us. The rapid evolution of digital platforms and technological advancements has transformed the landscape of media, reshaping the ways in which information is produced, disseminated, and consumed. This transformation has profound implications for individuals, communities, and societies, as media and technology play a pivotal role in shaping public discourse, cultural norms, and social dynamics.

The advent of the internet and the proliferation of digital devices have democratized access to information, enabling individuals to connect with others and engage with content from around the globe. This connectivity has fostered a more interconnected and informed society, where individuals can access diverse perspectives and engage in meaningful dialogue. However, the sheer volume of information available online presents challenges, as individuals must navigate a complex and often overwhelming digital landscape to discern credible sources and accurate information.

Social media platforms have emerged as powerful tools for communication and self-expression, allowing individuals to share their thoughts, experiences, and ideas with a global audience. These platforms have facilitated the rise of citizen journalism, where individuals can report on events and issues in real-time, challenging traditional media narratives and providing alternative perspectives. Social media has also played a crucial role in mobilizing social movements and fostering community engagement, as individuals and groups use these platforms to organize, advocate, and raise awareness about important issues.

Despite the benefits of social media, there are also significant challenges associated with its use. The spread of misinformation and disinformation on these platforms has become a pressing concern, as false or misleading information can quickly gain traction and influence public opinion. This phenomenon underscores the importance of media literacy, as individuals must develop the skills to critically evaluate the information they encounter and discern credible sources from unreliable ones. Media literacy education can empower individuals to navigate the digital landscape with confidence, fostering a more informed and discerning society.

The role of traditional media has also evolved in response to the rise of digital platforms and changing consumer habits. While traditional media outlets such as newspapers, television, and radio continue to play a significant role in shaping public discourse, they face increasing competition from digital-native platforms and independent content creators. This shift has prompted traditional media organizations to adapt their strategies, embracing digital technologies and exploring new formats to engage audiences and remain relevant in a rapidly changing media landscape.

Technology has also transformed the production and consumption of media content, enabling new forms of storytelling and creative expression. Advances in digital tools and platforms have democratized content creation, allowing individuals to produce and share their own media with a global audience. This democratization has given rise to a diverse array of voices and perspectives, enriching the media landscape and challenging traditional gatekeepers of information and culture.

The rise of streaming services and on-demand content has further transformed the media landscape, as consumers increasingly seek personalized and convenient access to entertainment and information. This shift has disrupted traditional models of media distribution and consumption, prompting media organizations to innovate and adapt to changing consumer preferences. The convergence of media and technology has also given rise to new forms of interactive and immersive content, such as virtual reality and augmented reality, offering audiences novel and engaging experiences.

As media and technology continue to evolve, they present both opportunities and challenges for individuals and societies. The potential for media and technology to foster greater connectivity, creativity, and engagement is immense, but it also requires careful consideration of ethical and social implications. Issues such as privacy, data security, and digital equity must be addressed to ensure that the benefits of media and technology are accessible to all individuals and communities.

The role of media and technology in shaping public discourse and cultural norms cannot be overstated. As individuals engage with media content and digital platforms, they are exposed to diverse perspectives and ideas that influence their beliefs, attitudes, and behaviors. This exposure can foster greater understanding and empathy, but it can also reinforce existing biases and stereotypes if not approached critically. Media and technology have the power to amplify marginalized voices and challenge dominant narratives, but they also have the potential to perpetuate harmful ideologies and misinformation.

To harness the potential of media and technology for positive change, individuals and organizations must prioritize ethical and responsible practices. This includes promoting media literacy education, supporting diverse and inclusive content, and advocating for policies that protect privacy and data security. By fostering a media landscape that values accuracy, transparency, and inclusivity, individuals and societies can navigate the complexities of the digital age with confidence and integrity.

Chapter 2

Cultural Identity and Governance

Defining Cultural Identity

Cultural identity is a complex tapestry woven from the threads of history, language, traditions, and beliefs that define a group of people. It is an intricate mosaic that shapes how individuals perceive themselves and their place in the world. This identity is not static; it evolves over time, influenced by internal dynamics and external interactions. Understanding cultural identity requires delving into the myriad factors that contribute to its formation and expression.

At the heart of cultural identity lies the concept of shared heritage. This encompasses the historical experiences, customs, and values passed down through generations. These elements serve as a foundation upon which cultural identity is built, providing a sense of continuity and belonging. For many, this shared heritage is a source of pride and a means of connecting with others who share similar backgrounds. It is through these connections that individuals find a sense of community and solidarity.

Language plays a pivotal role in shaping cultural identity. It is not merely a tool for communication but a vessel for conveying cultural nuances, values, and worldviews. Language carries with it the stories, idioms, and expressions unique to a culture, serving as a repository of collective memory. For individuals, speaking their native language can evoke a deep sense of identity and connection to their cultural roots. Conversely, the loss of language can lead to a sense of dislocation and cultural erosion.

Traditions and rituals are another cornerstone of cultural identity. These practices, often rooted in historical or religious significance, provide a framework for individuals to express their cultural identity. Whether through festivals, ceremonies, or daily customs, traditions offer a tangible link to the past and a means of reinforcing cultural values. They serve as a reminder of the shared experiences and beliefs that bind a community together, fostering a sense of continuity and belonging.

Beliefs and values are integral to cultural identity, shaping how individuals perceive the world and their place within it. These beliefs may be influenced by religion, philosophy, or societal norms, and they often guide behavior and decision-making. For many, cultural identity is closely tied to a set of core values that define what is considered right or wrong, acceptable or unacceptable. These values provide a moral compass, influencing how individuals interact with others and navigate the complexities of life.

Cultural identity is also shaped by external influences, as individuals and communities interact with other cultures. This interaction can lead to the exchange of ideas, practices, and values, enriching cultural identity and fostering a sense of global interconnectedness. However, it can also present challenges, as individuals navigate the tension between preserving their cultural heritage and adapting to new influences. This dynamic interplay between tradition and change is a hallmark of cultural identity, reflecting its fluid and evolving nature.

Migration and globalization have further complicated the landscape of cultural identity. As individuals move across borders and cultures intermingle, new hybrid identities emerge, blending elements from multiple cultural backgrounds. These hybrid identities challenge traditional notions of cultural identity, highlighting its dynamic and multifaceted nature. For individuals navigating these complex identities, the process of defining cultural identity can be both empowering and challenging, as they seek to reconcile diverse influences and forge a sense of self.

The role of cultural identity in shaping individual and collective experiences cannot be overstated. It influences how individuals perceive themselves and others, shaping their interactions and relationships. Cultural identity can be a source of strength and resilience, providing individuals with a sense of belonging and purpose. It can also be a source of conflict, as differing cultural identities come into contact and compete for recognition and acceptance.

In a world characterized by diversity and interconnectedness, understanding and respecting cultural identity is essential. It requires an openness to learning about and appreciating the rich tapestry of cultures that make up our global community. By embracing cultural diversity, individuals can foster greater empathy and understanding, bridging divides and building a more inclusive and harmonious society.

Cultural Identity in Policy Making

Policy making is a complex process that involves balancing diverse interests, addressing societal needs, and shaping the future of communities. Cultural identity plays a crucial role in this process, influencing how policies are developed, implemented, and perceived. Understanding the intersection of cultural identity and policy making is essential for creating inclusive and effective policies that resonate with the communities they aim to serve.

Cultural identity encompasses the shared heritage, language, traditions, beliefs, and values that define a group of people. It shapes how individuals perceive themselves and their place in the world, influencing their interactions with others and their engagement with societal structures. In the context of policy making, cultural identity can impact both the content of policies and the processes through which they are developed.

One of the key ways cultural identity influences policy making is through the representation of diverse voices and perspectives. Policymakers must consider the cultural identities of the communities they serve to ensure that policies are inclusive and equitable. This requires engaging with diverse stakeholders, including community leaders, cultural organizations, and individuals from various backgrounds. By incorporating diverse perspectives, policymakers can better understand the unique needs and priorities of different cultural groups, leading to more effective and culturally sensitive policies.

Cultural identity also plays a role in shaping the priorities and goals of policy making. Different cultural groups may have distinct values and beliefs that influence their views on issues such as education, healthcare, and social services. For example, a community that places a high value on family and community support may prioritize policies that strengthen social networks and provide resources for family caregivers. By understanding these cultural priorities, policymakers can develop policies that align with the values and aspirations of the communities they serve.

The implementation of policies is another area where cultural identity is significant. Policies that fail to consider cultural differences may face resistance or be less effective in achieving their intended outcomes. For instance, a public health campaign that does not account for cultural beliefs and practices related to health and wellness may struggle to gain traction in certain communities. To address this, policymakers must work to ensure that policies are culturally relevant and accessible, taking into account language barriers, cultural norms, and other factors that may impact their effectiveness.

Cultural identity can also influence the perception and acceptance of policies. Communities are more likely to support policies that reflect their cultural values and address their specific needs. Conversely, policies perceived as culturally insensitive or exclusionary may face opposition and undermine trust in government institutions. To build trust and foster community support, policymakers must engage in meaningful dialogue with cultural groups, demonstrating a commitment to understanding and respecting their identities.

The role of cultural identity in policy making extends beyond domestic contexts to the international arena. In an increasingly interconnected world, policymakers must navigate the complexities of cultural diversity on a global scale. This requires an awareness of cultural differences and an ability to engage in cross-cultural dialogue and collaboration. By fostering cultural understanding and cooperation, policymakers can address global challenges such as climate change, migration, and economic inequality in ways that respect and honor diverse cultural identities.

To effectively integrate cultural identity into policy making, policymakers must develop cultural competence—a set of skills and knowledge that enables them to understand, appreciate, and work effectively with individuals from diverse cultural backgrounds. This involves ongoing education and training, as well as a commitment to self-reflection and growth. By cultivating cultural competence, policymakers can enhance their ability to create policies that are inclusive, equitable, and responsive to the needs of all communities.

Incorporating cultural identity into policy making also requires a commitment to equity and social justice. Policymakers must recognize and address the systemic barriers and inequalities that disproportionately affect marginalized cultural groups. This involves examining the ways in which policies may perpetuate or exacerbate existing disparities and working to create policies that promote fairness and opportunity for all. By prioritizing equity and social justice, policymakers can contribute to a more inclusive and just society.

The integration of cultural identity into policy making is not without challenges. Policymakers must navigate the complexities of cultural diversity, balancing competing interests and addressing potential conflicts. This requires a willingness to engage in difficult conversations and a commitment to finding common ground. By approaching these challenges with empathy, openness, and a focus on shared goals, policymakers can work towards solutions that honor and respect cultural diversity.

Case Studies Cultural Identity in Action

In the vibrant tapestry of global society, cultural identity weaves its intricate patterns, influencing how communities interact, evolve, and thrive. Examining real-world examples provides valuable insights into how cultural identity manifests in various contexts, shaping outcomes and fostering understanding. Through these case studies, we can explore the dynamic interplay between cultural identity and societal development, highlighting both challenges and triumphs.

Consider the case of New Zealand, where the indigenous Māori culture plays a pivotal role in shaping national identity. The Treaty of Waitangi, signed in 1840 between Māori chiefs and the British Crown, serves as a foundational document that continues to influence contemporary policy and societal norms. Over the years, New Zealand has made significant strides in recognizing and integrating Māori culture into the national fabric. This is evident in the revitalization of the Māori language, which is now an official language of the country, and the incorporation of Māori customs and values into public institutions. The Waitangi Tribunal, established to address historical grievances, exemplifies the ongoing commitment to honoring Māori cultural identity and ensuring equitable representation. This case illustrates how acknowledging and embracing cultural identity can lead to more inclusive and harmonious societies.

In contrast, the experience of the Rohingya people in Myanmar highlights the devastating consequences of cultural identity being marginalized and suppressed. The Rohingya, a Muslim minority group, have faced decades of systemic discrimination and violence, culminating in a humanitarian crisis that has forced hundreds of thousands to flee their homes. The Myanmar government's refusal to recognize the Rohingya as citizens, coupled with widespread persecution, underscores the dangers of denying cultural identity and the resulting erosion of human rights. This case serves as a stark reminder of the importance of safeguarding cultural identity and promoting tolerance and acceptance to prevent conflict and suffering.

Turning to the Americas, the United States offers a complex mosaic of cultural identities, shaped by waves of immigration and the legacy of indigenous peoples. The city of Los Angeles, with its diverse population, exemplifies the rich interplay of cultural identities. Neighborhoods like Chinatown, Little Tokyo, and Olvera Street celebrate the heritage of their respective communities, contributing to the city's vibrant cultural landscape. However, this diversity also presents challenges, as seen in the tensions between different ethnic groups and the struggle for equitable access to resources and opportunities. Initiatives such as community-based organizations and cultural festivals play a crucial role in fostering dialogue and understanding, highlighting the potential for cultural identity to serve as a bridge rather than a barrier.

In Europe, the Basque Country in Spain provides a compelling example of cultural identity driving regional autonomy and self-determination. The Basque people, with their distinct language and cultural traditions, have long sought recognition and autonomy within Spain. The establishment of the Basque Autonomous Community, with its own parliament and control over key areas such as education and taxation, reflects the successful negotiation of cultural identity within a broader national framework. This case demonstrates how cultural identity can be a powerful force for political and social change, fostering a sense of pride and belonging while navigating the complexities of national unity.

The African continent offers a rich tapestry of cultural identities, each contributing to the continent's diverse heritage. In South Africa, the post-apartheid era has been marked by efforts to reconcile and celebrate the country's multicultural identity. The adoption of 11 official languages and the promotion of cultural diversity through initiatives like Heritage Day underscore the commitment to honoring the myriad cultural identities that make up the nation. The Truth and Reconciliation Commission, established to address the injustices of apartheid, serves as a testament to the power of acknowledging and embracing cultural identity in healing and rebuilding a divided society.

In Asia, the city-state of Singapore presents a unique model of multiculturalism, where cultural identity is both celebrated and managed within a highly structured framework. Singapore's government has implemented policies to promote racial harmony and integration, such as the Ethnic Integration Policy, which ensures a balanced mix of ethnic groups in public housing estates. Cultural festivals and events, like the Chingay Parade and Hari Raya celebrations, showcase the diverse cultural identities that coexist within the city. This case highlights the potential for cultural identity to be harnessed as a unifying force, fostering social cohesion and stability in a diverse society.

The experiences of indigenous communities in Canada offer valuable lessons in the recognition and preservation of cultural identity. The Truth and Reconciliation Commission of Canada, established to address the legacy of residential schools, has brought to light the importance of acknowledging and respecting indigenous cultural identities. Efforts to revitalize indigenous languages, protect traditional lands, and incorporate indigenous perspectives into education and governance reflect a growing commitment to honoring and preserving cultural identity. This case underscores the transformative potential of cultural identity in fostering reconciliation and healing.

In the Middle East, the Kurdish people have long sought recognition and autonomy, navigating complex political landscapes to assert their cultural identity. The establishment of the Kurdistan Regional Government in Iraq represents a significant achievement in the pursuit of self-determination, providing a platform for the preservation and promotion of Kurdish culture and language. This case illustrates the resilience and determination of cultural identity in the face of adversity, highlighting the enduring quest for recognition and empowerment.

Challenges in Multicultural Governance

Navigating the complexities of multicultural governance presents a unique set of challenges that require careful consideration and strategic planning. As societies become increasingly diverse, governments must adapt to the evolving needs of their populations, ensuring that all cultural groups are represented and respected. This task is far from straightforward, as it involves balancing competing interests, addressing historical grievances, and fostering social cohesion. By examining the intricacies of multicultural governance, we can better understand the obstacles faced by policymakers and the strategies employed to overcome them.

One of the primary challenges in multicultural governance is ensuring equitable representation for all cultural groups. In many countries, minority communities have historically been marginalized, leading to a lack of political power and influence. This can result in policies that do not adequately address the needs and concerns of these groups, perpetuating cycles of inequality and disenfranchisement. To address this issue, governments must implement measures to promote inclusivity and diversity within political institutions. This may involve adopting proportional representation systems, establishing advisory councils for minority communities, or implementing affirmative action policies to increase the participation of underrepresented groups in decision-making processes.

Another significant challenge is managing cultural tensions and conflicts that may arise within diverse societies. Differences in language, religion, and cultural practices can lead to misunderstandings and disputes, which, if left unaddressed, can escalate into larger societal conflicts. Governments must be proactive in fostering dialogue and understanding between cultural groups, promoting tolerance and acceptance as core societal values. This can be achieved through educational initiatives that emphasize multiculturalism, as well as community-building programs that encourage interaction and collaboration between different cultural communities.

The preservation of cultural heritage and identity is also a critical concern in multicultural governance. As societies modernize and globalize, there is a risk that traditional cultural practices and languages may be lost or diluted. Governments must strike a delicate balance between embracing progress and preserving cultural heritage, ensuring that all cultural groups have the opportunity to maintain their unique identities. This may involve supporting cultural festivals, funding language preservation programs, and protecting cultural sites and artifacts. By valuing and celebrating cultural diversity, governments can foster a sense of pride and belonging among all citizens.

Economic disparities between cultural groups pose another challenge in multicultural governance. In many cases, minority communities face higher levels of poverty and unemployment, limiting their access to resources and opportunities. Addressing these disparities requires targeted economic policies that promote equal access to education, employment, and healthcare. Governments must work to eliminate systemic barriers that contribute to economic inequality, such as discrimination in hiring practices or unequal access to quality education. By leveling the playing field, governments can empower all cultural groups to contribute to and benefit from economic growth.

Language barriers present a further obstacle in multicultural governance, as they can hinder communication and access to essential services. In multilingual societies, governments must ensure that all citizens can access information and services in their preferred language. This may involve providing translation and interpretation services, as well as producing official documents and communications in multiple languages. By prioritizing language accessibility, governments can enhance civic engagement and ensure that all cultural groups have equal access to public services.

The integration of immigrants and refugees into society is another complex issue that multicultural governance must address. Newcomers often face challenges in adapting to their new environment, including language barriers, cultural differences, and discrimination. Governments must implement policies that facilitate integration while respecting the cultural identities of immigrants and refugees. This may involve providing language and cultural orientation programs, supporting community organizations that assist newcomers, and promoting policies that combat discrimination and xenophobia. By fostering an inclusive environment, governments can help newcomers become active and valued members of society.

In addition to these challenges, multicultural governance must also contend with the impact of globalization and technological advancements. The rapid exchange of information and ideas across borders can both enrich and complicate cultural dynamics within societies. Governments must navigate the tension between embracing global influences and preserving local cultural identities. This may involve regulating media and technology to ensure diverse cultural representation, as well as supporting initiatives that promote cultural exchange and understanding.

The role of education in multicultural governance cannot be overstated. Schools play a crucial role in shaping the values and attitudes of future generations, making them a key arena for promoting multiculturalism and inclusivity. Governments must ensure that educational curricula reflect the diversity of society, incorporating the histories, languages, and cultures of all cultural groups. This can help foster mutual respect and understanding among students, preparing them to thrive in a multicultural world.

Finally, the success of multicultural governance depends on the active participation and engagement of all cultural groups. Governments must create opportunities for citizens to contribute to the decision-making process, ensuring that diverse perspectives are heard and considered. This may involve establishing forums for public consultation, supporting grassroots organizations, and promoting civic education and engagement. By empowering citizens to take an active role in governance, governments can build trust and legitimacy, fostering a sense of shared ownership and responsibility for the future of society.

The Balance Between Tradition and Progress

Striking a balance between tradition and progress is a delicate dance that societies have been performing for centuries. This intricate interplay shapes the cultural, social, and economic landscapes of communities worldwide. Tradition, with its deep roots and historical significance, provides a sense of identity and continuity. Progress, on the other hand, drives innovation and adaptation, propelling societies toward new horizons. The challenge lies in harmonizing these seemingly opposing forces to create a cohesive and dynamic society.

Tradition serves as the bedrock of cultural identity, offering a sense of belonging and continuity. It encompasses the customs, beliefs, and practices passed down through generations, forming the foundation upon which communities build their lives. These traditions often carry profound meaning, reflecting the values and wisdom of ancestors. They provide a sense of stability and comfort, anchoring individuals in a rapidly changing world. However, an unwavering adherence to tradition can sometimes stifle innovation and hinder societal growth.

Progress, characterized by innovation and change, is the driving force behind societal evolution. It encourages the exploration of new ideas, technologies, and ways of thinking, enabling societies to adapt to changing circumstances. Progress challenges the status quo, pushing boundaries and questioning established norms. It fosters creativity and problem-solving, leading to advancements in science, technology, and social structures. Yet, unchecked progress can lead to the erosion of cultural heritage and the loss of valuable traditions.

The tension between tradition and progress is evident in various aspects of society, from cultural practices to technological advancements. In many communities, traditional customs and rituals are being re-evaluated in light of modern values and lifestyles. For instance, traditional gender roles and family structures are being challenged by contemporary notions of equality and individualism. This shift can create friction between generations, as younger individuals seek to redefine their identities while respecting their cultural heritage.

In the realm of technology, the rapid pace of innovation presents both opportunities and challenges. Technological advancements have transformed the way people communicate, work, and interact with the world. While these changes have brought about significant benefits, they have also raised concerns about the impact on traditional ways of life. The rise of digital communication, for example, has altered social dynamics, with face-to-face interactions being replaced by virtual connections. This shift has implications for cultural practices that rely on personal interaction and community engagement.

Education plays a crucial role in navigating the balance between tradition and progress. Schools and educational institutions serve as bridges between the past and the future, imparting knowledge and values while encouraging critical thinking and innovation. By incorporating both traditional wisdom and modern perspectives, education can equip individuals with the tools needed to navigate a rapidly changing world. This approach fosters an appreciation for cultural heritage while promoting adaptability and resilience.

The arts also serve as a powerful medium for exploring the relationship between tradition and progress. Artists often draw inspiration from their cultural heritage, using traditional techniques and motifs to create contemporary works. This fusion of old and new allows for the preservation of cultural identity while embracing innovation and creativity. Through the arts, societies can celebrate their unique traditions while engaging with global influences and ideas.

In the realm of governance, policymakers face the challenge of balancing tradition and progress in their decision-making processes. This requires a nuanced understanding of the cultural, social, and economic contexts in which they operate. Policymakers must consider the potential impact of their decisions on cultural heritage and community values while promoting innovation and development. This delicate balancing act requires collaboration and dialogue between diverse stakeholders, ensuring that all voices are heard and respected.

The balance between tradition and progress is not a static equilibrium but a dynamic process that evolves over time. Societies must continuously reassess their priorities and values, adapting to new challenges and opportunities. This requires an openness to change and a willingness to engage in dialogue and reflection. By embracing both tradition and progress, societies can create a harmonious and inclusive environment that honors the past while embracing the future.

Chapter 3

Diversity in Political Systems

Understanding Diversity in Politics

Diversity in politics is a multifaceted concept that encompasses a wide range of perspectives, backgrounds, and experiences. It is a reflection of the broader society, where individuals from different ethnicities, genders, socioeconomic statuses, and ideologies come together to shape the political landscape. Understanding diversity in politics is crucial for fostering inclusive governance and ensuring that all voices are heard and represented in decision-making processes.

At its core, political diversity is about representation. It involves ensuring that elected officials and policymakers reflect the demographics and interests of the populations they serve. This representation is not limited to visible characteristics such as race or gender but extends to include diverse viewpoints and lived experiences. A diverse political landscape can lead to more comprehensive and equitable policies, as it allows for a broader range of perspectives to be considered in the legislative process.

One of the key benefits of diversity in politics is the potential for more innovative and effective solutions to complex societal challenges. When individuals from different backgrounds collaborate, they bring unique insights and approaches to problem-solving. This diversity of thought can lead to creative solutions that might not have been considered in a more homogenous environment. For example, policymakers from marginalized communities may have firsthand knowledge of the challenges faced by their constituents, enabling them to advocate for policies that address these issues more effectively.

Moreover, diversity in politics can enhance the legitimacy and credibility of democratic institutions. When citizens see themselves reflected in their political leaders, they are more likely to trust and engage with the political system. This sense of inclusion can lead to increased voter participation and civic engagement, strengthening the democratic process. Conversely, a lack of diversity in politics can lead to feelings of disenfranchisement and alienation among underrepresented groups, undermining the legitimacy of the political system.

Despite the clear benefits of diversity in politics, achieving it remains a significant challenge. Structural barriers, such as discriminatory practices, socioeconomic disparities, and unequal access to education and resources, can hinder the participation of marginalized groups in the political arena. Additionally, systemic biases and stereotypes can perpetuate the underrepresentation of certain groups, particularly women and minorities, in political leadership positions.

Efforts to promote diversity in politics often involve a combination of policy interventions, advocacy, and grassroots organizing. Electoral reforms, such as implementing proportional representation or establishing quotas for underrepresented groups, can help increase diversity in political institutions. These measures aim to create a more level playing field, ensuring that all individuals have an equal opportunity to participate in the political process.

Grassroots movements and advocacy organizations also play a crucial role in promoting diversity in politics. By raising awareness of the importance of representation and mobilizing communities to engage in the political process, these groups can help break down barriers to participation. They often work to empower individuals from marginalized communities, providing them with the tools and resources needed to run for office and advocate for their interests.

Education and mentorship are also essential components of efforts to increase diversity in politics. By providing training and support to aspiring political leaders from diverse backgrounds, mentorship programs can help build a pipeline of talent that reflects the diversity of society. These programs often focus on developing leadership skills, building networks, and navigating the political landscape, equipping individuals with the knowledge and confidence needed to succeed in politics.

The media also plays a significant role in shaping perceptions of diversity in politics. By highlighting the achievements and contributions of diverse political leaders, the media can challenge stereotypes and promote positive role models for underrepresented groups. However, media coverage can also perpetuate biases and reinforce negative stereotypes, underscoring the need for responsible and inclusive reporting.

Ultimately, understanding diversity in politics requires a commitment to inclusivity and equity at all levels of society. It involves recognizing the value of diverse perspectives and actively working to dismantle the barriers that prevent marginalized groups from participating in the political process. By fostering a more inclusive political landscape, societies can create a more just and equitable future for all citizens.

Representation and Inclusion

Representation and inclusion are foundational elements in the quest for a more equitable society. They are not mere buzzwords but essential components that ensure every individual has a voice and a place in the social, economic, and political fabric of a community. The journey toward achieving true representation and inclusion is complex, requiring a deep understanding of the barriers that exist and the strategies needed to overcome them.

At the heart of representation is the idea that all individuals, regardless of their background, should have the opportunity to participate in decision-making processes that affect their lives. This concept extends beyond mere presence; it involves active participation and influence. For representation to be meaningful, it must reflect the diversity of the population, encompassing various identities, experiences, and perspectives. This diversity enriches discussions and leads to more comprehensive and effective solutions to societal challenges.

Inclusion, on the other hand, is about creating environments where everyone feels valued and respected. It involves recognizing and addressing systemic inequalities that have historically marginalized certain groups. Inclusion is not just about bringing diverse individuals into a space but ensuring that they have equal access to opportunities and resources. It requires a commitment to equity, where the unique needs and contributions of each individual are acknowledged and supported.

One of the key challenges in achieving representation and inclusion is overcoming the structural barriers that have perpetuated inequality. These barriers can take many forms, including discriminatory policies, cultural biases, and socioeconomic disparities. For instance, in the workplace, women and minorities often face obstacles such as pay gaps, limited advancement opportunities, and a lack of mentorship. Addressing these issues requires a multifaceted approach that involves policy changes, cultural shifts, and targeted interventions.

Policy changes are a critical component of promoting representation and inclusion. Governments and organizations can implement measures such as affirmative action, diversity quotas, and anti-discrimination laws to level the playing field. These policies aim to create opportunities for underrepresented groups and ensure that they have a fair chance to succeed. However, policy changes alone are not enough; they must be accompanied by efforts to change cultural attitudes and behaviors.

Cultural shifts are necessary to challenge the stereotypes and biases that contribute to exclusion. This involves raising awareness about the value of diversity and fostering an environment where differences are celebrated rather than feared. Education plays a vital role in this process, as it can help individuals develop empathy and understanding for those who are different from themselves. By promoting diversity and inclusion in educational settings, societies can cultivate a new generation of leaders who are committed to equity and justice.

Targeted interventions are also essential for addressing the specific needs of marginalized groups. These interventions can take various forms, such as mentorship programs, leadership development initiatives, and community outreach efforts. Mentorship programs, for example, can provide guidance and support to individuals from underrepresented backgrounds, helping them navigate the challenges they may face in their careers. Leadership development initiatives can empower individuals to take on roles of influence and drive change within their communities.

Community outreach efforts are crucial for building bridges between different groups and fostering a sense of belonging. By engaging with diverse communities and listening to their needs and concerns, organizations can develop more inclusive policies and practices. This engagement also helps to build trust and collaboration, which are essential for creating lasting change.

Representation and inclusion are not static goals but ongoing processes that require continuous effort and reflection. They demand a willingness to listen, learn, and adapt to the evolving needs of society. As communities become more diverse, the importance of representation and inclusion will only continue to grow. By embracing these principles, societies can create environments where everyone has the opportunity to thrive and contribute to the common good.

The Impact of Diversity on Policy Outcomes

Diversity, in its many forms, has a profound impact on policy outcomes. It shapes the way policies are crafted, implemented, and perceived by the public. When diverse perspectives are included in the policy-making process, the resulting policies are more comprehensive, equitable, and effective. This chapter delves into the multifaceted ways in which diversity influences policy outcomes, highlighting the benefits and challenges associated with incorporating diverse voices into decision-making.

At the core of diversity's impact on policy is the idea that a wide range of perspectives leads to more robust and innovative solutions. When individuals from different backgrounds, cultures, and experiences come together to address a policy issue, they bring unique insights and ideas that might otherwise be overlooked. This diversity of thought can lead to creative problem-solving and the development of policies that are more responsive to the needs of a diverse population.

For example, consider a policy aimed at improving public health outcomes. A diverse policy-making team might include healthcare professionals, community leaders, and individuals from various socioeconomic backgrounds. Each member of the team brings their own experiences and expertise to the table, allowing for a more nuanced understanding of the health challenges faced by different communities. As a result, the policy is more likely to address the root causes of health disparities and promote equitable access to healthcare services.

Diversity also plays a crucial role in ensuring that policies are inclusive and equitable. When policy-makers represent a broad spectrum of society, they are more likely to consider the needs and concerns of marginalized and underrepresented groups. This inclusivity helps to prevent the creation of policies that inadvertently perpetuate inequality or discrimination. Instead, policies are designed to promote social justice and equal opportunities for all individuals, regardless of their background.

Moreover, diverse policy-making teams are better equipped to anticipate and address potential unintended consequences of policies. By considering a wide range of perspectives, policy-makers can identify potential pitfalls and challenges before they arise. This proactive approach helps to minimize negative impacts and ensures that policies are more effective in achieving their intended goals.

However, incorporating diversity into policy-making is not without its challenges. One of the primary obstacles is overcoming biases and stereotypes that may exist within the policy-making process. These biases can manifest in various ways, such as the exclusion of certain voices or the prioritization of certain perspectives over others. To address this issue, it is essential to create an environment where all voices are heard and valued. This requires a commitment to equity and inclusion, as well as ongoing efforts to challenge and dismantle systemic biases.

Another challenge is the potential for conflict and disagreement among diverse policy-making teams. When individuals with different perspectives come together, there is a risk of clashing opinions and priorities. However, these conflicts can be constructive if managed effectively. By fostering open communication and collaboration, policy-makers can harness the power of diversity to reach consensus and develop policies that reflect the collective wisdom of the group.

To maximize the benefits of diversity in policy-making, it is important to implement strategies that promote inclusivity and collaboration. One such strategy is to actively seek out and engage with diverse stakeholders throughout the policy-making process. This can be achieved through public consultations, focus groups, and community engagement initiatives. By involving a wide range of voices, policy-makers can gain a deeper understanding of the issues at hand and develop policies that are more attuned to the needs of the population.

Additionally, providing training and support for policy-makers can help to build their capacity to work effectively in diverse teams. This training can focus on topics such as cultural competency, unconscious bias, and conflict resolution. By equipping policy-makers with the skills and knowledge needed to navigate diversity, they are better prepared to create policies that are inclusive and equitable.

Barriers to Political Participation

Political participation is a cornerstone of democratic societies, yet numerous barriers can impede individuals from engaging fully in the political process. These obstacles can be structural, cultural, or personal, and they often intersect in complex ways. Understanding these barriers is crucial for fostering a more inclusive and representative political system. This chapter examines the various impediments to political participation, offering insights into their origins and potential solutions.

One of the most significant barriers to political participation is the structural limitations embedded within electoral systems. These can include restrictive voting laws, gerrymandering, and the disenfranchisement of certain groups. For instance, voter ID laws, while ostensibly designed to prevent fraud, can disproportionately affect marginalized communities, such as low-income individuals, racial minorities, and the elderly, who may face difficulties in obtaining the necessary identification. Similarly, gerrymandering, the practice of drawing electoral district boundaries to favor a particular party, can dilute the voting power of certain groups, effectively marginalizing their voices in the political process.

Another structural barrier is the complexity of the voting process itself. In many countries, the registration process can be cumbersome and confusing, deterring potential voters from participating. Additionally, the lack of accessible polling places and inconvenient voting times can further discourage individuals from casting their ballots. These logistical challenges are particularly pronounced for people with disabilities, those living in rural areas, and individuals with demanding work schedules.

Cultural barriers also play a significant role in limiting political participation. Societal norms and values can influence individuals' perceptions of their ability to effect change through political engagement. In some cultures, there may be a prevailing belief that politics is a domain reserved for the elite or that individual participation is unlikely to make a difference. This sense of political alienation can be exacerbated by a lack of representation in political institutions, where decision-makers often do not reflect the diversity of the population they serve.

Media representation and discourse can further entrench cultural barriers. When political coverage is dominated by sensationalism or biased reporting, it can create a distorted view of the political landscape, leading to disillusionment and apathy among potential voters. Moreover, the underrepresentation of certain groups in media narratives can perpetuate stereotypes and reinforce the notion that politics is not for everyone.

Personal barriers, such as socioeconomic status, education level, and language proficiency, also contribute to disparities in political participation. Individuals from lower socioeconomic backgrounds may face financial constraints that limit their ability to engage in political activities, such as attending rallies or donating to campaigns. Education level can influence political knowledge and awareness, with those having limited educational opportunities potentially feeling less informed and confident in their ability to participate.

Language proficiency is another critical factor, particularly in multicultural societies. For individuals who do not speak the dominant language fluently, accessing information about political issues and candidates can be challenging. This language barrier can hinder their ability to make informed decisions and participate fully in the political process.

Addressing these barriers requires a multifaceted approach that involves policy changes, community engagement, and education. One potential solution is to implement policies that make voting more accessible and convenient. This could include measures such as automatic voter registration, extended voting hours, and the provision of more polling places, particularly in underserved areas. Additionally, adopting alternative voting methods, such as mail-in ballots or online voting, could help to alleviate logistical challenges and increase participation.

Efforts to combat gerrymandering and ensure fair representation are also essential. Independent redistricting commissions, which draw electoral boundaries without political bias, can help to create more equitable districts and empower marginalized communities. Legal challenges and advocacy efforts can also play a role in addressing discriminatory voting laws and practices.

Cultural barriers can be addressed through initiatives that promote political engagement and representation. Encouraging diverse candidates to run for office and supporting grassroots movements can help to create a more inclusive political landscape. Media organizations also have a responsibility to provide balanced and accurate coverage, highlighting diverse voices and perspectives.

Education is a powerful tool for overcoming personal barriers to political participation. Civic education programs can equip individuals with the knowledge and skills needed to engage in the political process effectively. These programs can be integrated into school curricula and offered through community organizations, ensuring that individuals from all backgrounds have access to the information they need to participate.

Language barriers can be mitigated by providing multilingual resources and support. Governments and organizations can offer election materials and information in multiple languages, ensuring that non-native speakers have the opportunity to engage fully in the political process. Community outreach efforts can also play a role in bridging language gaps and fostering a sense of inclusion.

Strategies for Enhancing Diversity

Diversity is a multifaceted concept that encompasses a range of human differences, including race, ethnicity, gender, age, sexual orientation, disability, and more. In today's interconnected world, enhancing diversity is not just a moral imperative but also a strategic advantage. Organizations and communities that embrace diversity are better positioned to innovate, adapt, and thrive in an ever-changing environment. This chapter delves into strategies for enhancing diversity, offering practical guidance for individuals and institutions seeking to create more inclusive spaces.

One of the foundational strategies for enhancing diversity is fostering an inclusive culture. This involves creating an environment where all individuals feel valued, respected, and empowered to contribute their unique perspectives. An inclusive culture is built on the principles of equity and fairness, ensuring that everyone has access to the same opportunities and resources. To achieve this, organizations must actively challenge biases and stereotypes, both at the individual and systemic levels. This can be accomplished through diversity training programs that raise awareness and promote understanding among employees.

Leadership plays a crucial role in driving diversity initiatives. Leaders must demonstrate a genuine commitment to diversity by setting clear goals and holding themselves accountable for progress. This includes implementing policies and practices that support diversity, such as flexible work arrangements, mentorship programs, and diverse hiring practices. Leaders should also serve as role models, embodying the values of inclusivity and demonstrating how diversity can be leveraged for success.

Recruitment and retention are key components of any diversity strategy. To attract a diverse pool of candidates, organizations must broaden their recruitment efforts and actively seek out talent from underrepresented groups. This can involve partnering with educational institutions, community organizations, and professional networks that focus on diversity. Additionally, organizations should review their hiring processes to identify and eliminate any biases that may disadvantage certain candidates.

Retention is equally important, as it ensures that diverse talent remains within the organization and continues to contribute to its success. To retain diverse employees, organizations must create a supportive and inclusive work environment that encourages professional growth and development. This can include offering mentorship and sponsorship programs, providing opportunities for skill-building and advancement, and recognizing and rewarding contributions from all employees.

Another effective strategy for enhancing diversity is to promote diversity in leadership positions. Diverse leadership teams bring a wealth of perspectives and experiences, enabling organizations to make more informed and innovative decisions. To achieve this, organizations must actively identify and develop diverse talent, providing them with the resources and support needed to advance into leadership roles. This can involve offering leadership development programs, creating succession plans that prioritize diversity, and ensuring that diverse candidates are considered for leadership opportunities.

Collaboration and partnerships are also essential for enhancing diversity. By working together with other organizations, communities, and stakeholders, institutions can share best practices, resources, and insights to advance diversity initiatives. Collaborative efforts can include joint diversity training programs, community outreach initiatives, and advocacy efforts to promote diversity and inclusion at a broader level.

Data and metrics play a critical role in measuring progress and identifying areas for improvement. Organizations should collect and analyze data on diversity and inclusion, using it to inform decision-making and track the effectiveness of their diversity strategies. This can involve conducting regular diversity audits, setting measurable diversity goals, and reporting on progress to stakeholders. Transparency and accountability are key, as they demonstrate a commitment to continuous improvement and build trust with employees and the wider community.

Education and awareness are fundamental to enhancing diversity. By educating individuals about the value of diversity and the importance of inclusion, organizations can foster a more inclusive mindset and culture. This can involve offering diversity training programs, hosting workshops and seminars, and providing resources and materials that promote understanding and empathy. Education should be ongoing and integrated into the fabric of the organization, ensuring that diversity remains a priority at all levels.

Technology can also be leveraged to enhance diversity. Digital platforms and tools can facilitate communication and collaboration among diverse teams, enabling individuals to connect and share ideas across geographical and cultural boundaries. Technology can also be used to support diversity initiatives, such as virtual diversity training programs, online mentorship platforms, and data analytics tools that track diversity metrics.

Finally, it is important to recognize that enhancing diversity is an ongoing journey, not a destination. Organizations and individuals must remain committed to continuous learning and improvement, adapting their strategies as needed to address emerging challenges and opportunities. By embracing diversity and fostering an inclusive culture, organizations can unlock the full potential of their workforce and create a more equitable and just society.

Chapter 4

Identity and Political Movements

The Role of Identity in Political Activism

Identity plays a pivotal role in shaping political activism, serving as both a catalyst for mobilization and a framework for understanding social and political dynamics. At its core, identity encompasses the characteristics, beliefs, and affiliations that define individuals and groups. These elements of identity can include race, ethnicity, gender, sexual orientation, religion, nationality, and more. In the realm of political activism, identity not only influences the issues that individuals and groups choose to champion but also affects the strategies they employ and the alliances they form.

The intersection of identity and political activism is evident in the way marginalized communities have historically organized to advocate for their rights and interests. For many, political activism is a means of asserting their identity and challenging systems of oppression that have marginalized them. The civil rights movement in the United States, for example, was driven by the collective identity of African Americans who sought to dismantle racial segregation and discrimination. Similarly, the feminist movement has been propelled by the shared experiences and identities of women advocating for gender equality.

Identity can serve as a powerful motivator for political activism by fostering a sense of solidarity and shared purpose among individuals who identify with a particular group. This sense of belonging can inspire individuals to take action, whether through protests, advocacy, or other forms of activism. When people see their identity reflected in a movement, they are more likely to feel a personal stake in its success and to contribute their time, energy, and resources to its cause.

The role of identity in political activism is also evident in the way activists frame their messages and campaigns. By appealing to shared identities and experiences, activists can create narratives that resonate with their target audiences and galvanize support. This strategic use of identity can help movements gain visibility and legitimacy, as well as attract allies and supporters from outside the immediate community. For instance, the LGBTQ+ rights movement has successfully used identity-based messaging to highlight issues such as marriage equality and anti-discrimination protections, garnering widespread support and achieving significant policy changes.

However, the relationship between identity and political activism is not without its challenges. Identity can be a source of division as well as unity, particularly when different groups have competing interests or priorities. Within movements, tensions can arise when individuals or subgroups feel that their specific identities or concerns are not adequately represented or addressed. These internal conflicts can hinder the effectiveness of activism and undermine the cohesion of the movement.

Moreover, the emphasis on identity in political activism can sometimes lead to the exclusion of individuals who do not fit neatly into predefined categories. This can result in a narrow focus that overlooks the complexity and intersectionality of identities, where individuals may belong to multiple marginalized groups simultaneously. Activists must navigate these complexities and strive to create inclusive movements that recognize and embrace the diversity of identities within their ranks.

The digital age has further transformed the role of identity in political activism. Social media platforms and online communities have provided new avenues for individuals to express their identities and connect with like-minded activists. These digital spaces have facilitated the rapid dissemination of information and the organization of grassroots movements, enabling activists to reach a global audience and mobilize support across borders. The #MeToo movement, for example, harnessed the power of social media to amplify the voices of survivors of sexual harassment and assault, transcending geographical and cultural boundaries.

Despite the opportunities presented by digital activism, there are also challenges associated with the online representation of identity. The anonymity and reach of the internet can lead to the spread of misinformation and the amplification of divisive rhetoric. Activists must be vigilant in ensuring that their online presence accurately reflects their identities and values, while also countering harmful narratives that may arise.

In navigating the complexities of identity in political activism, it is essential for activists to engage in self-reflection and dialogue. By examining their own identities and biases, activists can better understand the perspectives and experiences of others, fostering empathy and collaboration. Open and honest conversations about identity can help bridge divides and build stronger, more inclusive movements.

Furthermore, activists must be willing to adapt and evolve their strategies in response to changing social and political landscapes. This may involve reevaluating the role of identity in their activism and exploring new ways to engage with diverse communities. By remaining flexible and open to new ideas, activists can ensure that their movements remain relevant and effective in addressing the needs and aspirations of their constituents.

Case Studies Identity-Driven Movements

The power of identity-driven movements lies in their ability to galvanize individuals around shared experiences, values, and goals. These movements often emerge from a deep-seated need to address systemic injustices and to assert the rights and dignity of marginalized communities. By examining case studies of such movements, we can gain valuable insights into the strategies, challenges, and successes that have defined their trajectories.

One of the most prominent identity-driven movements in recent history is the Black Lives Matter (BLM) movement. Born out of the frustration and anger over the systemic racism and police brutality faced by African Americans, BLM has become a global force for change. The movement's origins can be traced back to the acquittal of George Zimmerman in the shooting death of Trayvon Martin in 2013. The hashtag #BlackLivesMatter quickly gained traction on social media, serving as a rallying cry for those demanding justice and accountability.

BLM's success can be attributed to its decentralized structure, which allows for a diverse range of voices and perspectives to be heard. This inclusivity has enabled the movement to adapt and respond to the unique needs of different communities, while maintaining a unified message. By leveraging social media and digital platforms, BLM has been able to amplify its message and mobilize supporters across the globe. The movement's emphasis on intersectionality has also been crucial, as it acknowledges the interconnectedness of various forms of oppression and seeks to address them holistically.

Another compelling case study is the LGBTQ+ rights movement, which has made significant strides in advancing equality and acceptance for individuals of diverse sexual orientations and gender identities. The Stonewall Riots of 1969 are often cited as the catalyst for the modern LGBTQ+ rights movement. These spontaneous demonstrations, led by members of the LGBTQ+ community in response to a police raid at the Stonewall Inn in New York City, marked a turning point in the fight for LGBTQ+ rights.

The movement has since evolved into a powerful force for change, advocating for issues such as marriage equality, anti-discrimination protections, and transgender rights. One of the key strategies employed by the LGBTQ+ rights movement has been the use of personal narratives to humanize and destigmatize LGBTQ+ identities. By sharing their stories, individuals have been able to challenge stereotypes and misconceptions, fostering greater understanding and acceptance.

The LGBTQ+ rights movement has also been successful in building coalitions and alliances with other social justice movements. By recognizing the intersectionality of identities, the movement has been able to address the unique challenges faced by LGBTQ+ individuals who belong to other marginalized groups, such as people of color or those with disabilities. This collaborative approach has strengthened the movement and expanded its reach, resulting in significant legal and cultural victories.

The feminist movement provides another illuminating example of an identity-driven movement that has achieved transformative change. Rooted in the struggle for gender equality, the feminist movement has evolved through various waves, each characterized by distinct goals and strategies. The first wave, which emerged in the late 19th and early 20th centuries, focused on securing legal rights for women, such as the right to vote. The second wave, which gained momentum in the 1960s and 1970s, sought to address broader issues of gender inequality, including workplace discrimination, reproductive rights, and domestic violence.

The feminist movement's ability to adapt and evolve has been key to its longevity and success. By embracing a diverse range of voices and perspectives, the movement has been able to address the unique challenges faced by women of different races, ethnicities, and socioeconomic backgrounds. This inclusivity has been instrumental in fostering solidarity and building a broad-based coalition of supporters.

One of the defining features of the feminist movement has been its emphasis on consciousness-raising and education. By raising awareness of the systemic nature of gender inequality, the movement has been able to challenge deeply ingrained societal norms and attitudes. This focus on education has empowered individuals to advocate for change in their own communities, creating a ripple effect that has contributed to widespread social and cultural shifts.

The Indigenous rights movement is another powerful example of an identity-driven movement that has sought to address historical injustices and advocate for the rights and sovereignty of Indigenous peoples. This movement has been characterized by its emphasis on cultural preservation, land rights, and self-determination. One of the most notable successes of the Indigenous rights movement has been the recognition of Indigenous land rights and the return of ancestral lands in various countries.

The movement's strength lies in its ability to draw on the rich cultural heritage and traditions of Indigenous peoples, using these as a foundation for advocacy and activism. By asserting their identity and reclaiming their narratives, Indigenous activists have been able to challenge colonial legacies and demand justice and reparations. The movement has also been successful in building alliances with other social justice movements, recognizing the interconnectedness of struggles for justice and equality.

These case studies illustrate the diverse ways in which identity-driven movements have harnessed the power of identity to effect change. While each movement is unique in its goals and strategies, they share common themes of resilience, adaptability, and inclusivity. By embracing the complexity and intersectionality of identities, these movements have been able to build broad-based coalitions and achieve significant social, cultural, and legal victories.

The success of identity-driven movements also highlights the importance of storytelling and narrative in activism. By sharing personal experiences and highlighting the human impact of systemic injustices, activists can create powerful narratives that resonate with a wide audience. These stories have the potential to shift public opinion, influence policy, and inspire others to join the fight for justice.

Intersectionality and Its Influence

Intersectionality, a term coined by Kimberlé Crenshaw in 1989, has become a pivotal concept in understanding the complexities of identity and social justice. It refers to the interconnected nature of social categorizations such as race, class, gender, and sexuality, which can create overlapping and interdependent systems of discrimination or disadvantage. By examining how these identities intersect, we can gain a deeper understanding of the unique challenges faced by individuals who belong to multiple marginalized groups.

The influence of intersectionality is evident in various social movements and advocacy efforts. It has reshaped the way activists and scholars approach issues of inequality, emphasizing the need to consider the multifaceted experiences of individuals rather than viewing them through a single lens. This holistic perspective has led to more inclusive and effective strategies for addressing systemic injustices.

One of the key areas where intersectionality has had a profound impact is in the feminist movement. Traditional feminist discourse often centered on the experiences of white, middle-class women, overlooking the unique struggles faced by women of color, LGBTQ+ women, and women from lower socioeconomic backgrounds. Intersectionality has challenged this narrow focus, urging feminists to consider the diverse experiences of all women and to address the ways in which race, class, and other factors intersect with gender.

This shift has led to a more inclusive feminist movement that recognizes the importance of addressing issues such as racial discrimination, economic inequality, and LGBTQ+ rights alongside gender equality. By acknowledging the interconnectedness of these issues, feminists have been able to build stronger coalitions and advocate for more comprehensive policy changes that benefit all women.

Intersectionality has also played a crucial role in the fight for racial justice. The Black Lives Matter movement, for example, has embraced an intersectional approach by highlighting the unique challenges faced by Black women, LGBTQ+ individuals, and people with disabilities within the broader struggle against systemic racism. This inclusive approach has helped to amplify the voices of those who are often marginalized within their own communities, ensuring that their experiences and needs are not overlooked.

By centering the experiences of the most marginalized individuals, intersectionality has enabled activists to develop more nuanced and effective strategies for combating racial injustice. This approach has also fostered greater solidarity among different social justice movements, as activists recognize the interconnectedness of their struggles and work together to address the root causes of inequality.

In the realm of LGBTQ+ rights, intersectionality has been instrumental in highlighting the diverse experiences and challenges faced by individuals within the community. While the LGBTQ+ rights movement has made significant strides in recent years, it has often focused on the experiences of white, cisgender individuals, neglecting the unique struggles faced by LGBTQ+ people of color, transgender individuals, and those from lower socioeconomic backgrounds.

Intersectionality has encouraged LGBTQ+ activists to adopt a more inclusive approach, recognizing the importance of addressing issues such as racial discrimination, economic inequality, and gender identity alongside sexual orientation. This shift has led to a more comprehensive and effective movement that is better equipped to advocate for the rights and dignity of all LGBTQ+ individuals.

The influence of intersectionality extends beyond social movements and into the realm of policy and legislation. Policymakers and advocates are increasingly recognizing the importance of considering the intersecting identities of individuals when crafting policies and programs. This approach ensures that the unique needs and experiences of marginalized communities are taken into account, leading to more equitable and effective solutions.

For example, intersectional analysis has been used to inform policies related to healthcare, education, and criminal justice. By considering the ways in which race, gender, class, and other factors intersect, policymakers can develop targeted interventions that address the specific barriers faced by marginalized individuals. This approach not only leads to more effective policy outcomes but also helps to dismantle the systemic structures that perpetuate inequality.

Intersectionality has also influenced the way organizations and institutions approach diversity and inclusion. Many organizations are now adopting intersectional frameworks to better understand and address the unique challenges faced by their employees and stakeholders. This approach involves examining the ways in which various identities intersect and influence individuals' experiences within the organization, leading to more inclusive and equitable practices.

By embracing intersectionality, organizations can create environments that are more welcoming and supportive of diverse individuals. This not only benefits employees and stakeholders but also enhances the organization's overall effectiveness and success. Research has shown that diverse and inclusive organizations are more innovative, adaptable, and better equipped to meet the needs of their clients and customers.

The influence of intersectionality is also evident in the field of education. Educators and scholars are increasingly recognizing the importance of incorporating intersectional perspectives into their curricula and teaching practices. This approach involves examining the ways in which various identities intersect and influence individuals' experiences within educational settings, leading to more inclusive and equitable learning environments.

By adopting an intersectional approach, educators can better understand and address the unique challenges faced by marginalized students. This not only enhances the educational experience for all students but also helps to dismantle the systemic structures that perpetuate inequality within the education system. Intersectional education empowers students to think critically about the world around them and to advocate for social justice and equity in their own communities.

The influence of intersectionality is far-reaching and transformative. By challenging traditional approaches to identity and social justice, intersectionality has reshaped the way we understand and address issues of inequality. It has fostered greater inclusivity and solidarity among social justice movements, leading to more effective advocacy and policy outcomes.

Identity Politics and Social Change

Identity politics has emerged as a significant force in shaping social change, influencing the way individuals and groups advocate for their rights and recognition. At its core, identity politics involves organizing around shared aspects of identity—such as race, gender, sexuality, or religion—to address systemic inequalities and seek justice. This approach has been both celebrated for its ability to empower marginalized communities and critiqued for potentially fragmenting broader social movements. Understanding the dynamics of identity politics is crucial for comprehending its role in driving social change.

The roots of identity politics can be traced back to the civil rights movements of the 1960s and 1970s, when marginalized groups began to organize around their shared identities to demand equal rights and representation. The feminist movement, the LGBTQ+ rights movement, and the Black Power movement are all examples of identity-based organizing that sought to challenge the status quo and advocate for social justice. These movements highlighted the importance of recognizing and valuing diverse identities, paving the way for future generations to continue the fight for equality.

One of the key strengths of identity politics is its ability to give voice to marginalized communities that have historically been excluded from mainstream political discourse. By organizing around shared identities, individuals can amplify their voices and draw attention to the unique challenges they face. This has led to increased visibility and representation for marginalized groups, both in the political arena and in broader society.

For example, the LGBTQ+ rights movement has successfully used identity politics to advocate for legal and social recognition. By organizing around their shared identity, LGBTQ+ individuals have been able to push for significant policy changes, such as marriage equality and anti-discrimination protections. This has not only improved the lives of LGBTQ+ individuals but has also fostered greater acceptance and understanding within society as a whole.

Similarly, the Black Lives Matter movement has utilized identity politics to highlight the systemic racism and police violence faced by Black individuals. By centering the experiences of Black people, the movement has been able to draw attention to the urgent need for racial justice and reform. This has sparked important conversations about race and inequality, leading to increased awareness and action on these critical issues.

However, identity politics is not without its challenges. Critics argue that organizing around identity can lead to fragmentation and division within broader social movements. By focusing on specific identities, there is a risk of overlooking the interconnectedness of various forms of oppression and failing to build coalitions across different groups. This can hinder efforts to address systemic inequalities that affect multiple communities.

To address these challenges, it is essential for advocates of identity politics to adopt an intersectional approach. Intersectionality, as discussed in previous chapters, involves recognizing the ways in which different aspects of identity intersect and influence individuals' experiences. By considering the interconnectedness of race, gender, class, and other factors, advocates can develop more inclusive and effective strategies for social change.

For instance, the feminist movement has increasingly embraced intersectionality to address the diverse experiences of women from different backgrounds. By acknowledging the unique challenges faced by women of color, LGBTQ+ women, and women from lower socioeconomic backgrounds, feminists can work towards a more inclusive movement that addresses the needs of all women. This approach not only strengthens the movement but also fosters greater solidarity and collaboration among different social justice efforts.

In addition to adopting an intersectional approach, it is important for advocates of identity politics to engage in coalition-building and allyship. By working together with other marginalized groups, individuals can amplify their voices and build stronger movements for social change. This involves recognizing the shared struggles and goals of different communities and working collaboratively to address systemic inequalities.

For example, the Women's March, which began in 2017, brought together individuals from diverse backgrounds to advocate for a wide range of social justice issues, including gender equality, racial justice, and LGBTQ+ rights. By building coalitions across different identities, the march was able to draw attention to the interconnectedness of these issues and advocate for comprehensive policy changes that benefit all marginalized communities.

Allyship also plays a crucial role in advancing identity politics and social change. Allies are individuals who support and advocate for the rights of marginalized communities, even if they do not share the same identity. By using their privilege and influence to amplify the voices of marginalized individuals, allies can help to create more inclusive and equitable spaces.

For instance, straight allies have played an important role in advancing LGBTQ+ rights by advocating for policy changes and challenging discriminatory attitudes. Similarly, white allies have been instrumental in supporting the Black Lives Matter movement by using their privilege to draw attention to issues of racial injustice and advocate for systemic reform.

The role of identity politics in social change is complex and multifaceted. While it has the potential to empower marginalized communities and drive significant progress, it also presents challenges that must be navigated carefully. By adopting an intersectional approach, engaging in coalition-building, and fostering allyship, advocates can harness the power of identity politics to create meaningful and lasting social change.

Criticisms and Controversies

Criticisms and controversies are inherent to any movement or ideology that seeks to challenge established norms and provoke change. As society evolves, so too do the debates surrounding the methods and impacts of these movements. Understanding the criticisms and controversies that arise is essential for navigating the complex landscape of social change and for refining strategies to achieve desired outcomes.

One of the most prominent criticisms leveled against social movements is the accusation of divisiveness. Critics argue that by focusing on specific identities or issues, movements can inadvertently create rifts within society, pitting groups against one another rather than fostering unity. This criticism is often directed at identity-based movements, where the emphasis on particular identities can be perceived as exclusionary or as prioritizing one group's needs over another's. The challenge lies in balancing the need for focused advocacy with the broader goal of societal cohesion.

Another common controversy involves the tactics employed by social movements. Activists often face scrutiny for their methods, whether they involve peaceful protests, civil disobedience, or more confrontational approaches. Critics may argue that certain tactics are too disruptive or alienating, potentially undermining public support for the movement's goals. However, history has shown that disruptive tactics can be effective in drawing attention to urgent issues and in compelling those in power to respond. The key is to assess the context and potential impact of different tactics, weighing the risks and benefits to determine the most effective course of action.

The role of social media in modern activism has also sparked debate. On one hand, social media platforms have democratized access to information and provided a powerful tool for organizing and amplifying voices. Movements can quickly gain momentum and reach a global audience, raising awareness and mobilizing support. On the other hand, the rapid spread of information can lead to misinformation, oversimplification of complex issues, and the potential for online harassment or backlash. Navigating the digital landscape requires a strategic approach, ensuring that messaging is accurate, inclusive, and constructive.

Funding and resource allocation present another area of controversy. Movements often rely on donations, grants, and other forms of financial support to sustain their activities. Critics may question the sources of funding, particularly if they come from corporate or political entities with vested interests. Transparency and accountability in financial matters are crucial for maintaining credibility and trust within the movement and among its supporters. Additionally, the allocation of resources can be contentious, as different factions within a movement may have competing priorities or visions for how funds should be used.

The intersection of social movements with political systems is another point of contention. While some movements choose to work within existing political frameworks to achieve change, others may reject these systems altogether, viewing them as inherently flawed or oppressive. This divergence in approach can lead to internal conflicts and debates over the most effective path to achieving social justice. Engaging with political systems can offer opportunities for policy change and institutional reform, but it also requires navigating complex power dynamics and potential compromises.

Critics also raise concerns about the potential for co-optation or dilution of movement goals. As movements gain visibility and influence, there is a risk that their messages may be appropriated or watered down by mainstream entities seeking to capitalize on their popularity. This can lead to a loss of authenticity and a divergence from the movement's original objectives. To counteract this, movements must remain vigilant in preserving their core values and ensuring that their messaging remains true to their mission.

The question of representation and leadership within movements is another source of controversy. Ensuring diverse and inclusive leadership is essential for reflecting the varied experiences and perspectives of those the movement seeks to represent. However, achieving this can be challenging, particularly in movements with a long history or established hierarchies. Striking a balance between experienced leadership and fresh voices is crucial for fostering innovation and adaptability while maintaining continuity and stability.

The impact of social movements on public opinion and policy is a subject of ongoing debate. While some movements achieve significant victories, others may struggle to effect lasting change. Critics may point to perceived failures or setbacks as evidence of a movement's ineffectiveness, while supporters may argue that progress is incremental and that even small gains are meaningful. Evaluating the success of a movement requires a nuanced understanding of its goals, strategies, and the broader social and political context in which it operates.

Despite these criticisms and controversies, social movements remain a vital force for change. They challenge entrenched power structures, raise awareness of pressing issues, and inspire individuals to take action. By engaging with and addressing criticisms, movements can refine their strategies, build stronger coalitions, and enhance their impact. Constructive dialogue and critical reflection are essential for navigating the complexities of social change and for ensuring that movements remain responsive to the needs and aspirations of those they seek to serve.

In the face of criticism, it is important for movements to remain adaptable and open to feedback. This involves actively listening to diverse perspectives, engaging in self-reflection, and being willing to evolve in response to changing circumstances. By fostering a culture of inclusivity and collaboration, movements can build resilience and sustain momentum in the pursuit of their goals.

Chapter 5

Global Perspectives on Identity Politics

Identity Politics Across Continents

Identity politics, a term that has gained significant traction in recent decades, refers to the political stances and movements that arise from the shared experiences and interests of specific social groups. These groups often form around characteristics such as race, ethnicity, gender, sexual orientation, religion, or nationality. The concept of identity politics is not confined to any single region or culture; rather, it manifests in diverse ways across continents, reflecting the unique historical, social, and political contexts of each area.

In North America, identity politics has been a driving force in shaping the political landscape, particularly in the United States and Canada. The civil rights movement of the 1960s laid the groundwork for subsequent identity-based movements, including those advocating for women's rights, LGBTQ+ rights, and Indigenous rights. These movements have sought to address systemic inequalities and discrimination, often challenging the dominant narratives and power structures. In recent years, the Black Lives Matter movement has brought renewed attention to issues of racial injustice and police brutality, highlighting the ongoing struggle for racial equality.

In Latin America, identity politics is deeply intertwined with the region's colonial history and the legacy of European conquest. Indigenous movements have been at the forefront of identity-based activism, advocating for land rights, cultural preservation, and political representation. Countries like Bolivia and Ecuador have seen significant Indigenous political mobilization, with leaders like Evo Morales and Rafael Correa championing Indigenous rights and incorporating Indigenous perspectives into national policies. Additionally, Afro-Latinx communities have organized to combat racial discrimination and promote cultural recognition, drawing attention to the intersectionality of race and identity in the region.

Europe presents a complex tapestry of identity politics, shaped by its diverse cultures, languages, and histories. The European Union's emphasis on multiculturalism and integration has both fostered and challenged identity-based movements. In countries like France and Germany, debates over immigration and national identity have sparked tensions, with far-right parties capitalizing on fears of cultural erosion. Meanwhile, movements advocating for the rights of ethnic minorities, such as the Roma and Kurdish populations, continue to push for greater inclusion and recognition. The rise of feminist and LGBTQ+ movements across Europe has also highlighted the continent's evolving understanding of identity and equality.

In Africa, identity politics is often linked to the continent's colonial past and the arbitrary borders drawn by colonial powers. Ethnic and tribal identities play a significant role in political dynamics, with some countries experiencing tensions and conflicts rooted in these divisions. However, identity politics in Africa is not solely defined by ethnic lines. Movements advocating for gender equality, LGBTQ+ rights, and religious freedom have gained momentum, challenging traditional norms and advocating for social change. South Africa's post-apartheid era, for example, has seen a focus on racial reconciliation and the empowerment of marginalized communities.

Asia's vast and diverse landscape presents a wide array of identity politics, influenced by cultural, religious, and historical factors. In India, caste-based politics remains a significant force, with movements advocating for the rights of Dalits and other marginalized groups. The country's complex religious landscape also shapes identity politics, with tensions between Hindu and Muslim communities influencing political discourse. In China, ethnic minority groups such as the Uighurs and Tibetans face challenges in preserving their cultural identities within a dominant Han Chinese framework. Meanwhile, LGBTQ+ movements in countries like Japan and Taiwan are gaining visibility, advocating for legal recognition and social acceptance.

The Middle East, with its rich tapestry of cultures and religions, is no stranger to identity politics. Sectarian divisions, particularly between Sunni and Shia Muslims, have historically influenced political dynamics in countries like Iraq and Lebanon. The region's diverse ethnic groups, including Kurds, Arabs, and Persians, also navigate complex identity politics, often in the context of state-building and national identity. Women's rights movements in the

Middle East have gained traction, challenging patriarchal norms and advocating for greater gender equality in both legal and social spheres.

Oceania, encompassing Australia, New Zealand, and the Pacific Islands, presents a unique context for identity politics. Indigenous movements, such as those of the Aboriginal and Torres Strait Islander peoples in Australia and the Māori in New Zealand, have been instrumental in advocating for land rights, cultural preservation, and political representation. These movements have sought to address the historical injustices of colonization and promote reconciliation and recognition. Additionally, the Pacific Islands face identity politics related to climate change, as rising sea levels threaten their very existence and cultural heritage.

Across continents, identity politics serves as a powerful tool for marginalized groups to assert their rights, challenge systemic inequalities, and advocate for social change. While the specific issues and contexts may vary, common themes emerge, such as the struggle for recognition, representation, and equality. Identity politics can be both a unifying force, bringing together individuals with shared experiences, and a source of tension, as different groups navigate competing interests and priorities.

Critics of identity politics argue that it can lead to fragmentation and division, emphasizing differences rather than commonalities. However, proponents contend that acknowledging and addressing the unique experiences and challenges faced by marginalized groups is essential for achieving true equality and justice. By centering the voices and perspectives of those who have historically been excluded or marginalized, identity politics seeks to create a more inclusive and equitable society.

Comparative Analysis of Governance Models

Governance models, the frameworks through which societies organize authority and decision-making, vary widely across the globe. Each model reflects the unique historical, cultural, and political contexts of its region, offering distinct approaches to managing public affairs. By examining these models, we can gain insights into their strengths, weaknesses, and adaptability in addressing contemporary challenges.

Democracy, a governance model characterized by the participation of citizens in decision-making processes, is prevalent in many parts of the world. It operates on principles of representation, accountability, and the rule of law. In representative democracies, elected officials act on behalf of the people, making decisions that reflect the electorate's preferences. This model is lauded for its ability to incorporate diverse perspectives and adapt to changing societal needs. However, it is not without its challenges. Issues such as voter apathy, political polarization, and the influence of money in politics can undermine democratic processes, leading to questions about the true representativeness of elected bodies.

In contrast, authoritarian governance models concentrate power in the hands of a single leader or a small group. These regimes often justify their centralized control by emphasizing stability, efficiency, and national security. While authoritarian models can swiftly implement policies and maintain order, they often do so at the expense of individual freedoms and political dissent. The lack of accountability mechanisms can lead to abuses of power and corruption, as seen in various historical and contemporary examples. Despite these drawbacks, some authoritarian regimes have achieved significant economic growth and development, raising questions about the trade-offs between political freedom and economic progress.

Hybrid governance models, which combine elements of democracy and authoritarianism, have emerged in several countries. These systems often feature democratic institutions, such as elections and parliaments, alongside authoritarian practices, such as media censorship and restricted civil liberties. Hybrid models can offer a semblance of democratic legitimacy while maintaining centralized control. However, they also face criticism for undermining democratic principles and perpetuating authoritarian tendencies. The balance between democratic and authoritarian elements in hybrid models can vary widely, reflecting the unique political dynamics of each country.

Federalism, a governance model that divides power between central and regional authorities, is another approach to managing public affairs. This model allows for regional autonomy and accommodates diverse cultural, linguistic, and ethnic identities within a single nation. Federal systems can promote innovation and experimentation, as regional governments tailor policies to local needs. However, federalism can also lead to conflicts over jurisdiction and resource allocation, as well as disparities in governance quality across regions. The effectiveness of federal systems often depends on the clarity of constitutional arrangements and the willingness of central and regional authorities to cooperate.

In contrast, unitary governance models concentrate power in a central authority, with regional or local governments exercising limited autonomy. This model can facilitate uniform policy implementation and reduce administrative complexity. However, it may also struggle to accommodate regional diversity and address local needs effectively. Unitary systems often rely on strong central leadership to maintain cohesion and ensure equitable resource distribution. The success of unitary models depends on the ability of central authorities to balance national priorities with regional interests.

Traditional governance models, rooted in indigenous and customary practices, offer alternative approaches to managing public affairs. These models often emphasize consensus-building, communal decision-making, and respect for cultural traditions. Traditional governance can provide a sense of identity and continuity, fostering social cohesion and resilience. However, these models may face challenges in adapting to modern political and economic contexts, particularly when confronted with external pressures and influences. The integration of traditional governance with formal state structures can offer opportunities for innovation and inclusivity, but it also requires careful negotiation and mutual respect.

The effectiveness of any governance model depends on its ability to adapt to changing circumstances and address the needs of its citizens. In an increasingly interconnected world, governance models must navigate complex challenges, such as globalization, technological advancements, and environmental sustainability. The capacity for innovation, flexibility, and collaboration is crucial in ensuring that governance models remain relevant and responsive.

Comparative analysis of governance models reveals that no single model is universally superior. Each model has its strengths and weaknesses, shaped by the specific contexts in which it operates. The success of a governance model often hinges on its ability to balance competing interests, manage resources effectively, and foster social cohesion. By learning from the experiences of different governance models, countries can identify best practices and adapt them to their unique circumstances.

The interplay between governance models and societal values is also a critical factor in their effectiveness. Governance models that align with the cultural, historical, and social values of a society are more likely to gain legitimacy and support. Conversely, models that clash with societal values may face resistance and struggle to achieve their objectives. Understanding the cultural underpinnings of governance models can provide valuable insights into their strengths and limitations.

In the face of global challenges, such as climate change, pandemics, and economic inequality, governance models must also prioritize international cooperation and collaboration. The interconnected nature of these challenges requires coordinated efforts and shared solutions. Governance models that foster dialogue, build trust, and promote collective action are better positioned to address these complex issues.

The Influence of Globalization

Globalization, a multifaceted phenomenon, has reshaped the world in profound ways, influencing economies, cultures, and societies. Its impact is felt across borders, transcending geographical and political boundaries, and creating a more interconnected global community. The influence of globalization is evident in various aspects of life, from the way we communicate and conduct business to the cultural exchanges that enrich our societies.

One of the most significant effects of globalization is the integration of economies. The flow of goods, services, capital, and labor across borders has accelerated economic growth and development in many regions. Countries have become more interdependent, relying on each other for resources, technology, and markets. This economic integration has led to increased trade and investment, fostering innovation and competition. However, it has also created challenges, such as economic inequality and the vulnerability of local industries to global market fluctuations.

The rise of multinational corporations is a testament to the economic influence of globalization. These corporations operate in multiple countries, leveraging global supply chains to optimize production and distribution. They have the power to shape markets, influence consumer behavior, and drive technological advancements. While multinational corporations contribute to economic growth and job creation, they also raise concerns about corporate accountability, environmental sustainability, and the erosion of local cultures.

Globalization has also facilitated the exchange of ideas and cultural practices, leading to greater cultural diversity and understanding. The proliferation of digital communication technologies has made it easier for people to connect and share information across the globe. Social media platforms, online forums, and virtual communities have become spaces for cultural exchange, allowing individuals to learn about different traditions, languages, and perspectives. This cultural interconnectedness can foster tolerance and empathy, but it can also lead to cultural homogenization and the loss of unique cultural identities.

The influence of globalization extends to the political sphere, where it has reshaped governance and international relations. Global challenges, such as climate change, terrorism, and pandemics, require coordinated efforts and collective action. International organizations, treaties, and agreements have emerged to address these issues, promoting cooperation and dialogue among nations. However, globalization has also sparked debates about national sovereignty, as countries navigate the tension between global governance and domestic interests.

Technological advancements have been both a driver and a product of globalization. The rapid development of information and communication technologies has transformed the way we live and work, enabling real-time communication and access to information. The digital revolution has created new opportunities for innovation, entrepreneurship, and education, but it has also raised concerns about data privacy, cybersecurity, and the digital divide. As technology continues to evolve, its role in shaping globalization will remain a critical area of focus.

The environmental impact of globalization is another important consideration. The increased movement of goods and people has contributed to environmental degradation, including pollution, deforestation, and climate change. Globalization has also facilitated the spread of environmentally harmful practices, such as overfishing and unsustainable agriculture. Addressing these environmental challenges requires international cooperation and the adoption of sustainable practices that balance economic growth with environmental stewardship.

Globalization has had a profound impact on labor markets, influencing employment patterns and working conditions. The demand for skilled labor has increased, leading to greater opportunities for education and professional development. However, globalization has also contributed to job displacement and wage stagnation in certain industries, as companies seek to reduce costs through outsourcing and automation. The rise of the gig economy and remote work are examples of how globalization is reshaping the nature of work, offering flexibility and autonomy but also raising questions about job security and workers' rights.

The influence of globalization on education is evident in the growing emphasis on global competencies and cross-cultural understanding. Educational institutions are increasingly incorporating international perspectives into their curricula, preparing students to navigate a globalized world. Study abroad programs, international collaborations, and online learning platforms have expanded access to education and fostered global citizenship. However, disparities in educational access and quality remain a challenge, highlighting the need for equitable and inclusive educational opportunities.

Globalization has also played a role in shaping public health, as the movement of people and goods has facilitated the spread of diseases and health innovations. The COVID-19 pandemic underscored the interconnectedness of global health systems and the importance of international cooperation in addressing health crises. Globalization has enabled the rapid dissemination of medical knowledge and technologies, improving healthcare outcomes and access. However, it has also highlighted the vulnerabilities of global supply chains and the need for resilient health systems.

The influence of globalization on migration is a complex and multifaceted issue. Economic opportunities, political instability, and environmental factors drive people to migrate across borders in search of better lives. Migration has contributed to cultural diversity and economic growth in host countries, but it has also raised challenges related to integration, social cohesion, and border security. The experiences of migrants and their contributions to society are an integral part of the globalization narrative, reflecting the dynamic and interconnected nature of the world.

Identity Conflicts and Resolutions

Identity conflicts are a pervasive aspect of human experience, often arising from the complex interplay of personal, cultural, and societal influences. These conflicts can manifest in various forms, such as internal struggles with self-perception, clashes between cultural identities, or tensions within communities. Understanding the roots of identity conflicts and exploring potential resolutions is crucial for fostering harmony and personal growth.

At the heart of identity conflicts lies the question of self-definition. Individuals often grapple with the challenge of reconciling different aspects of their identity, such as ethnicity, nationality, gender, and religion. These elements can sometimes be at odds with one another, leading to confusion and inner turmoil. For instance, a person of mixed heritage may struggle to find a sense of belonging, feeling torn between two cultures. Similarly, someone who identifies as LGBTQ+ may face conflicts between their sexual orientation and societal or familial expectations.

Cultural identity conflicts can also arise when individuals or groups encounter differing values, beliefs, and practices. In an increasingly globalized world, people are exposed to diverse cultures and perspectives, which can lead to misunderstandings and tensions. For example, immigrants may experience identity conflicts as they navigate the challenges of adapting to a new culture while preserving their cultural heritage. These conflicts can be exacerbated by societal pressures to assimilate or conform to dominant cultural norms.

Societal identity conflicts often emerge from historical injustices, power imbalances, and systemic discrimination. Marginalized communities may face identity conflicts as they strive for recognition and equality within a society that has historically oppressed them. These conflicts can manifest in movements for social justice, as individuals and groups seek to assert their identity and demand change. The struggle for civil rights, gender equality, and indigenous rights are examples of societal identity conflicts that have shaped history and continue to influence contemporary discourse.

Resolving identity conflicts requires a multifaceted approach that addresses both individual and collective dimensions. On a personal level, self-reflection and introspection are essential for understanding the sources of identity conflict and developing a coherent sense of self. Engaging in open and honest dialogue with oneself can help individuals reconcile conflicting aspects of their identity and embrace their unique identity narrative. This process may involve exploring one's values, beliefs, and experiences, as well as seeking support from trusted friends, family, or mental health professionals.

Cultural identity conflicts can be addressed through intercultural dialogue and education. By fostering mutual understanding and respect, individuals and communities can bridge cultural divides and find common ground. This may involve creating spaces for cultural exchange, where people can share their traditions, stories, and perspectives. Educational initiatives that promote cultural awareness and sensitivity can also play a vital role in reducing cultural identity conflicts and promoting inclusivity.

Societal identity conflicts require systemic change and collective action. Addressing the root causes of these conflicts involves challenging discriminatory practices, policies, and structures that perpetuate inequality and exclusion. Advocacy and activism are powerful tools for raising awareness and driving change, as individuals and groups work together to dismantle oppressive systems and promote social justice. Building alliances and coalitions across diverse communities can amplify voices and create a united front in the pursuit of equality and recognition.

Empathy and active listening are crucial components of resolving identity conflicts. By seeking to understand the experiences and perspectives of others, individuals can foster a sense of connection and solidarity. This involves being open to different viewpoints, acknowledging the validity of others' experiences, and engaging in constructive dialogue. Empathy can help break down barriers and build bridges, creating an environment where diverse identities are valued and respected.

Identity conflicts can also be addressed through creative expression and storytelling. Art, literature, music, and other forms of creative expression provide powerful platforms for individuals to explore and communicate their identity narratives. By sharing their stories, individuals can challenge stereotypes, raise awareness, and inspire change. Creative expression can also serve as a means of healing and empowerment, allowing individuals to reclaim their identity and assert their place in the world.

In the context of identity conflicts, it is important to recognize the dynamic and evolving nature of identity. Identity is not static; it is shaped by experiences, relationships, and societal influences. Embracing this fluidity can help individuals navigate identity conflicts with greater flexibility and resilience. By acknowledging that identity is a journey rather than a fixed destination, individuals can approach conflicts with an open mind and a willingness to adapt and grow.

Lessons from International Case Studies

Examining international case studies offers a wealth of insights into the complexities of global issues and the diverse strategies employed to address them. These case studies serve as valuable learning tools, providing practical lessons that can be applied across various contexts. By analyzing the successes and challenges faced by different countries, we can gain a deeper understanding of the factors that contribute to effective problem-solving and policy implementation.

One notable case study is the transformation of Singapore from a developing nation to a global economic powerhouse. In the 1960s, Singapore faced significant challenges, including high unemployment, limited natural resources, and a lack of infrastructure. However, through visionary leadership and strategic planning, the country embarked on a journey of rapid development. Key to Singapore's success was its emphasis on education and skills development, which equipped its workforce to meet the demands of a changing economy. Additionally, the government implemented policies to attract foreign investment, foster innovation, and maintain political stability. Singapore's experience underscores the importance of long-term planning, investment in human capital, and the creation of a conducive environment for economic growth.

Another instructive case study is the approach taken by Denmark in addressing climate change and transitioning to a sustainable energy system. Denmark has emerged as a global leader in renewable energy, with wind power accounting for a significant portion of its electricity generation. This achievement is the result of a comprehensive energy policy that prioritizes sustainability and innovation. Denmark's success can be attributed to several factors, including strong political commitment, public-private partnerships, and community engagement. The Danish government set ambitious targets for reducing carbon emissions and invested in research and development to advance renewable technologies. Furthermore, Denmark's emphasis on public participation and consensus-building has fostered widespread support for its energy transition. This case study highlights the importance of setting clear goals, fostering collaboration, and engaging stakeholders in the pursuit of sustainable development.

The experience of Rwanda in post-conflict reconstruction and reconciliation offers valuable lessons in peacebuilding and social cohesion. Following the devastating genocide in 1994, Rwanda faced the daunting task of rebuilding its society and healing deep-seated divisions. The Rwandan government implemented a range of initiatives aimed at promoting unity and reconciliation, including the establishment of community-based justice systems known as Gacaca courts. These courts provided a platform for truth-telling, accountability, and forgiveness, allowing communities to address past grievances and move forward. Additionally, Rwanda prioritized economic development and poverty reduction as key components of its reconstruction efforts. By investing in infrastructure, education, and healthcare, the country has made significant strides in improving the quality of life for its citizens. Rwanda's experience underscores the importance of addressing the root causes of conflict, promoting inclusive governance, and fostering economic opportunities as part of a comprehensive peacebuilding strategy.

The case of Finland's education system provides valuable insights into the factors that contribute to high-quality education and student success. Finland consistently ranks among the top-performing countries in international assessments of student achievement. This success is attributed to a holistic approach to education that emphasizes equity, teacher professionalism, and student well-being. Finnish schools prioritize individualized learning, allowing students to progress at their own pace and receive support tailored to their needs. Teachers in Finland are highly trained and respected professionals, with a strong emphasis on continuous professional development. Furthermore, the Finnish education system fosters a culture of trust and collaboration, with minimal standardized testing and a focus on formative assessment. This case study highlights the importance of investing in teacher quality, promoting student-centered learning, and creating a supportive educational environment.

The response of South Korea to the COVID-19 pandemic offers important lessons in crisis management and public health. South Korea's approach was characterized by rapid and decisive action, extensive testing and contact tracing, and effective communication with the public. The government leveraged technology to implement a comprehensive testing and tracing system, which enabled the early detection and isolation of cases. Public health authorities provided clear and transparent information, fostering public trust and compliance with preventive measures. South Korea's experience demonstrates the importance of preparedness, agility, and effective communication in managing public health crises. It also underscores the value of leveraging technology and data to inform decision-making and enhance response efforts.

The case study of New Zealand's approach to indigenous rights and cultural preservation provides insights into the importance of recognizing and respecting indigenous communities. New Zealand has made significant progress in acknowledging the rights of the Māori people and promoting their cultural heritage. The Treaty of Waitangi, signed in 1840, serves as a foundational document for the relationship between the Māori and the New Zealand government. Efforts to honor the treaty have included land settlements, cultural revitalization programs, and the incorporation of Māori perspectives into national policy. New Zealand's experience highlights the importance of honoring historical agreements, promoting cultural diversity, and fostering partnerships with indigenous communities.